# of Long Ago

In the Museum

Long before people lived on Earth, there were many kinds of animals. The best place to find out what these animals looked like is a museum.

In some museums, the bones of prehistoric animals have been joined up to form complete skeletons (right).

You can also find fossils of small animals, like the one below.

Ammonite

Fossils

Fossils are the bones or shells of early animals preserved in rock.

The pictures on the right show how, over millions of years, an Icthyosaur turned into a fossil.

The insect, below, is also a fossil. It became trapped in a blob of resin. The resin hardened into amber and preserved the insect.

A dead animal falls to the seabed.

Soon, only the skeleton is left.

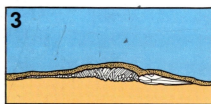

The skeleton is buried under layers of mud.

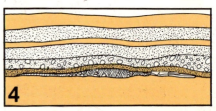

The mud turns to rock.

When scientists find pieces of rock with fossils inside, they cover them in Plaster of Paris. This protects the fossils, and stops them moving about. In the museum, the plaster is removed (right).

The bottom picture shows scientists digging out fossilised bones of elephants.

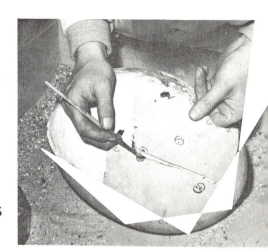

The Beginnings of Life

How life began is still a mystery. The first animals lived in the sea.

On the right is the fossil of a eurypterid (you-rip-ter-id). This sea animal looked like a scorpion.

Trilobites lived on the seabed. They used their legs for swimming.

Jellyfish

Sponges

Trilobites

Sea Lilies

Brachiopods

Eurypterid

Sea snails, jellyfish, and sponges lived in the sea.

Some cephalopods (sef-al-o-pods) had shells four metres long. They were cousins of the octopus.

Over millions of years, new kinds of animals developed.

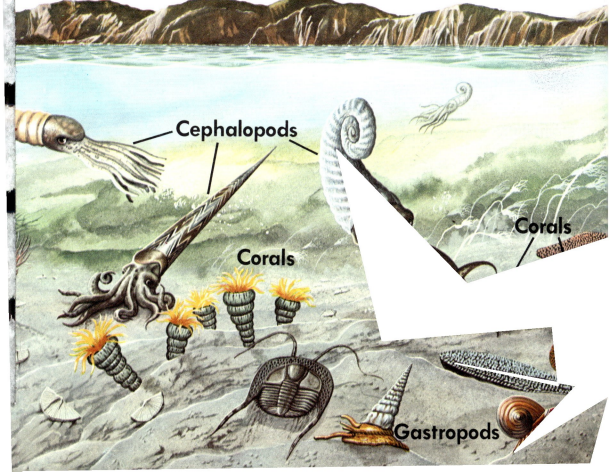

Cephalopods

Corals

Corals

Gastropods

The First Land Animals

Some of the new animals had backbones, which the early creatures did not.

From these new animals, the first land animals developed. These were amphibians. Amphibians can live on land or in water.

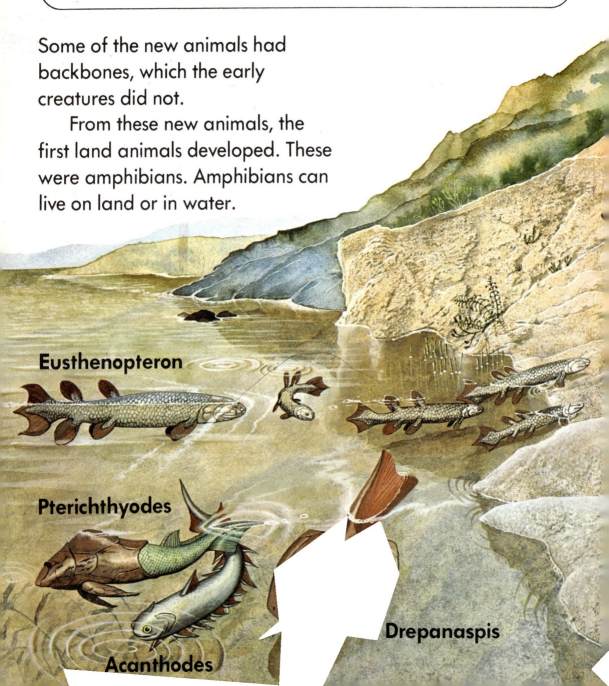

Eusthenopteron

Pterichthyodes

Acanthodes

Drepanaspis

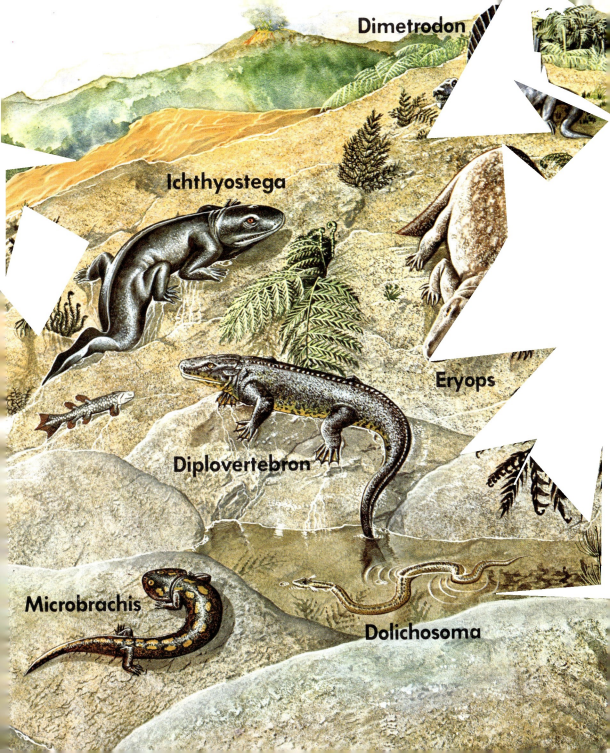

Dimetrodon

Ichthyostega

Eryops

Diplovertebron

Microbrachis

Dolichosoma

The Dinosaurs

After the amphibians came the reptiles. These are 'cold blooded' animals. Dinosaurs are the best-known of the early reptiles.

Brachiosaurus is the largest land animal that ever lived.

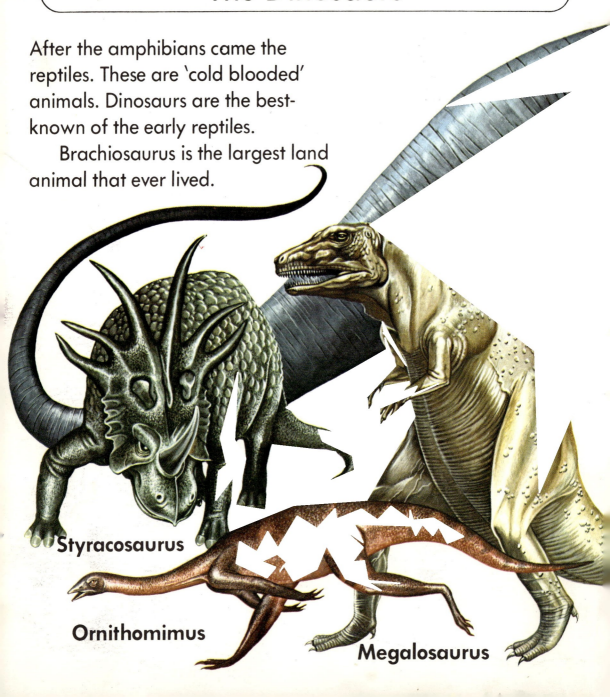

Styracosaurus

Ornithomimus

Megalosaurus

Diplodocus

13

Corythosaurus

Stegosaurus

How Dinosaurs Lived

Like all reptiles, dinosaurs laid eggs. Some dinosaurs ate plants. Others ate meat. The meat-eating dinosaurs were vicious fighters.

Sometimes, dinosaurs' footprints have been preserved (left) when the mud turned to rock.

Brontosaurus

Scolosaurus

Iguanodon

Tyrannosaurus

Triceratops

Protoceratops

Flying Reptiles

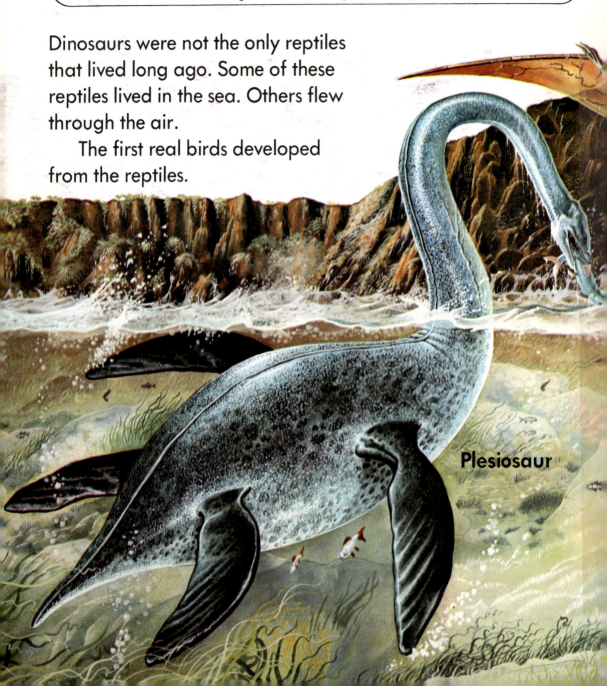

Dinosaurs were not the only reptiles that lived long ago. Some of these reptiles lived in the sea. Others flew through the air.

The first real birds developed from the reptiles.

Plesiosaur

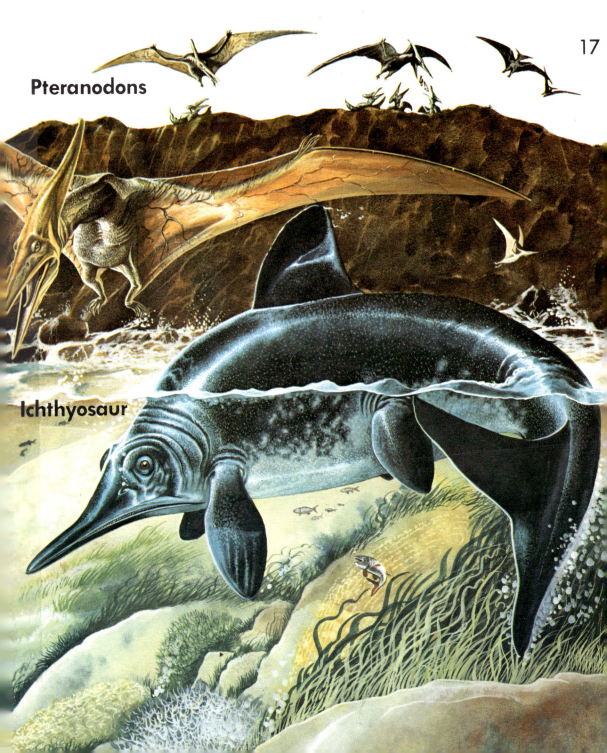

Pteranodons

Ichthyosaur

Early Mammals and Birds

Taeniolabis

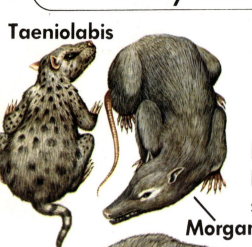

Mammals are warm-blooded creatures. The first mammals lived before the dinosaurs died out.

Most of these early mammals have also died out. Some kinds, however, such as the kangaroo, can still be found today.

Morganucodon

Phororhacos

Diprotodon

Giant Kangaroo

Diatryma

The first elephant was not much bigger than a modern pig.

Uintatherium had three pairs of horns on its head.

The modern horse has developed from Hyracotherium, an animal no bigger than a fox.

Alticamelus

Baluchitherium

Deinotherium

Smilodon

Hyracotherium

Uintatherium

The Ice Age

The Ice Age was a long period when
it was often very cold. The animals
that roamed the frozen lands had
thick woolly coats to keep them
warm.

Woolly Mammoths

Bison

Woolly
Rhinoceros

Wolf

It was not cold all over the world during the Ice Age. Some places were warmer than they are today.

Animals that lived in warm lands included rhinoceroses and lions.

Straight-tusked Elephants

Giant Deer

Rhinoceros

Lion

Glossary

Amber   Fossilised yellowish resin of pine trees.

Amphibian   An animal equally at home in the water or on land.

Brachiopod   A shellfish, sometimes called a Lampshell, that is now rare. It is often found as a fossil.

Brachiosaurus   The largest land animal that ever lived. Its name means 'arm lizard'.

Cephalopods   A group of sea creatures that includes ammonites. They are related to octopuses.

Dinosaurs   A group of reptiles that are now extinct. The name means 'terrible lizard'.

Eurypterid   An extinct water animal that varied in size from ten centimetres to two met

Fossils   The preserved remains of anim

Mammal   A warm-blooded animal wi

Mammoth   An extinct woolly elephan

Museum   A building where objects of are studied, conserved and displayed.

Reptile   A cold-blooded animal that l

Stegosaurus   A dinosaur with a thick name means 'roof lizard'.

Trilobites   A large group of extinct se varied in size from six millimetres to 75